700P207

S0-BEP-511

# PEOPLE, PLACES, PERSONAL

BY THE SAME AUTHOR

*Biography and Criticism*

The Nature of Biography
Young Thomas Hardy
The Older Hardy
John Keats
John Keats: The Living Year
The Odes of Keats
The Mask of Keats
The Keats Inheritance

*Plays and Poems*

Collected Poems
The Makers of Violence
Out of this Wood
Wentworth Place
Famous Meeting
This Tower My Prison
Matters of Love and Death
American Journey

# ROBERT GITTINGS

*People, Places, Personal*

SECKER & WARBURG
*LONDON*

First published in England 1985 by
Martin Secker & Warburg Limited
54 Poland Street, London W1V 3DF

Copyright © Robert Gittings 1985

British Library Cataloguing in Publication Data

Gittings, Robert
 People, places, personal.
 I. Title
 821'.912     PR6013.19

ISBN 0–436–17980–6

Typeset by Inforum Ltd, Portsmouth
Printed in England by
Redwood Burn Ltd, Trowbridge

To Leslie Norris

## ACKNOWLEDGEMENTS

Acknowledgements are due to the following publications: *Contemporary Review, Encounter, Envoi, New Poetry 1980, New Statesman, Night Ride to Sunrise, Outposts, Places, Poems for Charles Causley, Poetry South East 1979, Stand, Strawberry Fare, Thames Poetry.*

A Bursary from the Southern Arts Association enabled me to complete this book.

# CONTENTS

*People*

# FRANCES HOROVITZ, READER

She often said, while waiting
In the wings, to begin
And take the stage, or in
Some ill-kept dressing-room,
As if she were debating
Life, or inviting doom,

How she would so much rather
Not show herself at all,
Not answer to the call,
But only to be heard,
Bodiless like the weather
Or like an unseen bird.

Perfecting all she did,
She seems at length fulfilled
As if the end unwilled
Had come to answer choice,
Her presence to be hid,
Herself purely a voice.

# PUSHKIN

Prefiguring his own end, the poet composes
Lenski's aria, a puzzled résumé
Of death by duel. He sees the schoolroom where,
Twenty-sixth in class, the register
Commends his fencing and his verse-making.
He hears again the whispers and the jeers,
His too-broad nostrils, swarthy octoroon blood,
The shrugging shoulders of the dazzling ball-rooms,
The long assemblies walled with Baltic amber,
The white-bladed women. Plotting against the regime
Was commonplace, a young man's gesture: but,
To avoid Siberia, burn all papers, accept
Official exile not so far from Ovid,
Like him, banished into poetry, a locust
Nibbling the foliage of society. Hailed
The Russian Byron, uneasy toleration,
An insect to be crushed if the word came.
They got him through his wife, the beauty, insult,
A faked-up quarrel, hint of negro strain,
Some mystery about the pistols, and he
Was dead, the outsider, while the icy Czars
Ruled in their imperturbable palaces,
Until, eight decades more, the mob broke in,
Thick-lipped, half-savage peasants, staring, discovering,
Among the gold leaf that had cost their lives,
The desperate courage of the poet's words.

# HAWK IN A HOOD

Hawk-headed, an Egyptian
Wall-strip in profile, a strange man
To know, they said. One day he would
Claim you in boisterous, clamant mood,
The next, unrecognising, burrow,
Dull hunted partridge in clod furrow,
As if he shuddered at the gun
Loud friendship shouldered: an odd one,
They said, to know. To penetrate
The snow-storm of that blinded state
Neither his wife, mistress, nor friends
Could find the path where darkness ends
In lighter dark. A masking shroud
Shut him away, hawk in a hood.

# JOHN CLARE WALKS OUR LANE

Stout like John Clare, a broad-set country face,
He walks the lane he wandered as a child,
Puzzled, stumping along with stiff-legged pace,
Still, in that head, visions unreconciled
And regnant since the day his angel came
Sweeping across the pasture, a plumed wing
That flailed the senses out of him like flame,
Leaving him to be put away, screaming.

Released each week-end to his sisters' care
He stamps, all weathers, to the village shop,
Sweets and tobacco and a word to share
With unreflecting folk, who would not stop
To see his angel, though it waits, still there,
All weekday in those walls that hold no hope.

# CAVENDISH

Who set off to sail round the world
with two ships, named *Desire* and *Content*

*

Two ships set out,
*Desire, Content.*
To sail about
The world they went.

Two years were past;
*Desire* returned;
Canvas and mast
With glory burned.

Oceans away,
On some wild coast,
The waters' prey,
*Content* was lost.

Histories recall
This sole event;
*Desire* gained all,
But lost *Content.*

# CONTEMPORARIES

Schubert and Keats never one moment left
Composing, knowing how quickly death would come,
Their days on fire with life's Promethean theft.

Nussdorferstrasse and the Hampstead home,
Birthplace and dwelling, became a modern shrine.
We learn the legends of their equal doom,

Think of them both, drinking the same red wine,
Quite unaware how close their works were kin.

# ANCESTRAL PORTRAIT

*Headmaster, Keighley Grammar School*

He stares across my study, assured, cool,
In snow-white bands and well-cut clergy coat,
Headmaster of West Riding grammar school,
Son of the mill, whose father leased him out
To College learning and Victorian rote,
The social spiral from the whizzing spool
To the fine linen gathered at his throat,
A race of dalesmen tamed to his stern rule,

While up the moor, a maggot in his head,
The old, wild preacher fired his pistols, prayed
Beside his one boy on the drug-crazed bed,
Death in those walls a wildfell denizen,
And from a world not yet to print betrayed
Three pale, strange daughters signed their books as men.

# STRANGE VOYAGE

Samuel Taylor Coleridge, bound abroad,
Cabined with two fellow-passengers, hardly human,
A blotch-veined drunk on half-pay bed and board,
And a fat female of such gross monstrosity
'I think I never saw so large a woman,'
The poet wrote, calling her 'Mrs. Carnosity'.

And what did *they* think of the poet, who
Made the small cabin echo with dreadful screams,
His night-attacks from opium that drew
Pictures too horrible for sleep to check?
How could they guess in his disordered dreams
The unseen albatross hanging from his neck?

# CLASSIC ACTRESS

(after a production of *All's Well*)

From Juliet through to the Countess, fifty years
Have not worn out the everlasting flint,
All that warm movement, gesture, speech, still hers;
Of time's dismissive prompting not a hint.

Crossing a room, sitting, moving a chair,
Her simplest action appears total command,
Bodying the background of each character
Who leaves the wings where they in waiting stand.

After the applause, she takes a taxi, quits
The theatre, saying her good-nights at the door;
Lifetime of many lives her own completes,
Being herself the whole of them, and more.

# DYING WOMAN

Distress calls like a damaged bird
Continually she makes.
The repetition of a word
Is all that life partakes.

Is it a syllable of love
Or sanctuary from fear?
No ready watcher can remove
The dark wing hovering here.

# MADMAN ON THE BUS

The smiling madman talks on the top of the bus
To another invisible self, who answers and laughs
And agrees, with winks and nods, that the world is not
What it was. If you do not look you think two men
Are there. If you do look, you wonder if you yourself
Are deluded, so ready the dialogue and response.
Now medical welfare lets madmen walk the street
And jump on transport, confusions will be common,
Which side is which, of the threadline that divides
The sane creator from the creative insane.
Yet what with the addicts, and those people blurred
By alcohol, perfectly safe traditionalists,
The world is much as it was; it only seems strange
To us because of the bus, not adjusted to madmen.

# THE CHINESE INTERPRETER

Are you happy? Not since I was a child.
When did it stop? Directly I left school.
When was that? A dozen years ago.
Did you marry? Yes, at twenty-eight.
Why so late? It is the time allowed.
Is your home here? No, thousands of miles away
North, in Peking. And you work in Canton –
Any children? One boy. How old? Two months.
Is he like you? I have not seen him yet.
When will you see him? Next Spring Festival.
Only then can Chinese people travel.
When will that be? Three months more, in March.
And are you happy? I have told you. No.

His sad eyes blur through curtains of blind snow.

# GILBERT WHITE AT SELBORNE

Busy Mr. White, the Vicar's assistant,
Lived on family property for thirty years;
Nothing to do but enter his notebooks,
Making mild experiments with mice (one mouse
Scales just one ounce of lumping weight),
Dissecting birds, brought him by neighbours
And catapult boys, observing the habits
Of rare and common. The swallows worried him.
Did they or did they not migrate southward?
His brother had seen them in Spain by thousands,
But he himself, when Proctor at Oriel,
Watched them clinging to buildings in December –
Did they then hibernate in favoured cornices?
So filling his day with like speculations,
Writing to friends with nice exactness
Of birds, plants, reptiles, mammals – the cat
That fostered a leveret, the horse and hen
United in amity, a dell where echoes,
Rebounding, preferred quick, classical dactyls –
He tottered away like his own old tortoise,
Earthing its dark hybernaculum for winter.
Was death a migration or a hibernation?
Providence, benevolent as he believed,
Prints his pages, oddly immortal.

# CULTURAL REVOLUTION

He told me in the station underpass,
Where echoes would deceive an eavesdropper
Like high-tuned hearing-aids in crowded rooms,
His story of degradation: how the Red Guards
Beat his white-haired professor and himself,
Destroyed their being, threw them like spattered dung
To spread the fields. All his struggle then
Not to die starved was stamped across his cheeks,
Tight drawn, and his sunk chest and febrile cough:
Quoted Keats's *To Autumn* with a thin smile,
While floating mahogany leaves fell in the lake.
We said farewell in nervous haste. I went
By train to Shanghai, out of his hemisphere,
My copy of Keats pressed to his shrunken jacket.

# DUSTMEN

A pirate crew in comic dress,
Smee, Starky, Hook and Co.,
They hump away our household mess
Which else would never go.

As in defiance of their jobs
They heave the loads of trash,
Kingfisher-brilliant in their robes
Original and brash.

Their cheerful weekly visit brings
A chance that we may trust
Some respite in decay of things,
A light touch to our dust.

# THOMAS HARDY IN THE COW-SHED

(During a recent fuel crisis, it was stated
that there was probably not a labourer in
Wessex who knew how to milk by hand.)

*

Hither hieing in westernmost Wessex I fared me to find
Whether truly existless the hands that were heretofore wonted
To wring from its pendulous store the prime meal of mankind,
As when erstwhile I haunted.

Where domiciled formerly damsels of generous mien,
Albeit of rude genealogy, now in each shed
Was nought but the coil and the moil of the dinning machine,
Dairy wenches all dead,

Nay worse, fled to towns, where they flaunted and prinked them
so pert
No more womanly modest in watering place and parade,
In the latest of London adornings, each robe void of skirt,
And ruined each maid.

Till I cried, 'O immanent Unpurposeness, is this thy will?'
When started from out of the mirk in the midst of the byre
An ancient-smocked cowman, in cunning-wise milking them
still,
With hands caked in mire.

'Who *are* you?' I lipped; but his visage of elderly grizzle
Rebuked my misprision, 'Who *was* I were meeter for them
Who view thus my ghost! Go, visit my tomb where they chisel
"Thomas Hardy, O.M." '

*Places*

# VISITING WUSIH LAKE IN AUTUMN

(for Charles Causley)

One great bronze maple leaf spins down from the bough.
Square copper sails catch the lake's to-and-fro.
Flotilla islands glide beside us now
Till day recedes in evening's whispering flow.

Transient between two worlds, we travel through
Two beats of the heart's divided yes-and-no,
Seeing beyond the rose-reflected glow
The separation and the coming snow.

# ARKWRIGHT'S WATER POWER

The roaring valleys cut between gritstone cliffs,
And the shaking, shrieking waterwheels, turning, turning,
While wagons of frightened children from the sinks
Of Sheffield, the starvation workhouses,
Saw the hills clamp down a giant fist,
The overseers waiting at dusk with whips,
Not all bad, but all their authority
Bent to wring profit from those infant bodies,
No running away where there was nowhere to run.
So now the children of their children's grandchildren
Walk stiff-legged, board-chested, pelican-backed.
Yet they survived, though maimed, more than the wheel
And the apprentice houses of their prison.
Water, a casual tyrant, refused the thirst
Of the machinery. The engine house
Stands derelict by the river, where the kingfisher
Clips light and low, skimming the rushy stream.
The master died, a knighthood to his name,
And nameless children whisper at his gravestone,
Like water-sprites, haunting the fickle water.

# THE RAINMAKERS

These little goblets drained by parching time
Are drought-cups. When the rains refused to come,
The women gathered at the cliff-top head,
Where the old temple was, and wept their tears
Into these cups. Small bowls for the young girls
But larger measures for the old, who have
More sorrows, and can therefore bring more tears,
To weep until they brimmed the empty bowl,
And then the rains would hiss and leap, the priests
Promised. Now that their sanctuary is fallen
Into the sea, one finds a tiny cup
Wedged in a crevice just above high-water,
Sometimes even a greater, almost whole,
An ancient weeping nothing will control.

# LENINGRAD CUSTOM

At Peter's statue the bronze Czar
Rides, defying the Neva flood,
The wind blows from the Finland Gulf,
Chrysanthemums shake their buffeted heads.
Beside the monument's granite plinth,
One by one, stop bridal cars.

Young Russia's Saturday afternoon
Breaks from its work for wedding day.
They pose for photos at the foot,
The metal horseman rides on high,
A custom each one knows about,
And follows as the rest have done,

And then, the camera clicked, each bride
Takes a long stem from her bouquet
And lays it on the sloping base
Till, like an unofficial fete,
The colour climbs the rocky face
To where the armoured tyrant rides.

Ordinary couples leave their mark,
Silent as flowers upon the stone,
For all the despots keep their sway.
The one day's festival briefly gone,
The old street-cleaners bring away
Armfuls of blossom after dark.

# BYRON IN HUCKNALL

In Hucknall see Lord Byron stop,
Not in the church where he is laid,
But life-size in his statue, made
Over the doors of the Co-op,

Quizzing the crowds that come and go,
Poetic robes, Regency throat,
Open-necked shirt and loose cravat.
The busy check-out hums below.

Elegant lace ruffles his wrist,
A Grecian lyre is poised above.
By eloquence he tried to move
Mercy for those in want dismissed.

So now, sardonic, he surveys
A nation poorer than it knows,
Deprived of his defiant pose,
Lacking the freedom of his gaze.

# SPRING, WEST AND EAST

Chalk dust ribbons away.
Flints' lopsided faces
Jag the white-violet bank
Where the first butterfly floats.
Tractors corduroy turf
In broad, brown, sillion stripes.
Cloud-shapes cross the valley
And mount, the bramble shivers
Though still in sunshine, below
In larches the rooks, above
The lark's thrown clods, a potter's
Haphazard clay, to wheel
And drop the shape of a bird.
A semi-world away
One-quarter the human strain
Hoes the self-dunged field
Where the dun buffalo suckles,
Peach trees, pink in the stream,
Frame the reflected mountain,
Hacked rivulets run silver,
Squat blue-quilted children
Stagger, lifting their bales,
Under the yoke, men, women,
Trot with running shuffle
The breakback distance ordained,
Venturing a flat, creased smile
For the peak-nosed stranger, standing
Speechless but mortal too.

# SIEGE

Suppose headquarters had been Hampton Court,
Generals jackbooted stamping the State rooms,
Pictures vanished where master-thieves resort –
Brazil or Berchtesgaden's catacombs –
The statues target-split, the formal maze
Splintered for firewood, and, at final withdrawal,
The buildings mined for one revengeful blaze,
A rubble palace, London to appal.

Suppose a simple act of substitution,
For London read the name of Leningrad,
Phoenix of forty years from conflagration,
Roseate brick restored where millions bled:
A country that has never known invasion
Cannot imagine such resilient dead.

## LANDSCAPE WITH FIGURES: CORNWALL

Patter of overheard talk,
Shingle dashed against glass,
Foam over inland fields,
White blobs in blowing night,
Dipping and floating in flocks
Like moonmen landing on earth
Under a herringbone cloud
With startrail threading between –
Half memory and half dream,
The singular timing of love,
Extinct as the smoking, powdery,
Dust of a tufa cone,
Yet red, returning, to flash
Headland's revolving beam,
Catching the pair that embrace,
Transfixed, a landscape with figures.

# THE BELLS TOLL

'The bells tolled for death when I was a boy . . .
the years of the dead person's age would be tolled.'

When the bell stopped
At eighteen or twenty
A hush would come over
The fields, and the people
At plough or at harvest
Would stop too a moment,
Picturing the dead young
Man or woman, and
Seeing them living, in
Childhood or schooltime,
Or walking the aisle
Of early marriage,
Remote from an end,
A life at beginning
Of day, untouched by
Time and the bell,
The unfilled silence
And terror of noon.

# CATHEDRAL IN THE MARSHES, TORCELLO

Marble on the lagoon,
The lost cathedral rides
At mooring, ship of stone.

Sea-lavender, the tides
Pattern the netted walls,
While not a soul abides

Among the slim canals.
Where once a city stood
Empty reflection falls.

The market's multitude
Drowns in the liquid eye
Of silent desuetude.

Swallows rightangle by
Corners once populous,
And all that did not die

Is faith's deserted house,
To which we bring our love,
Echoing back to us

All that could live and move.

# OF MOOSE AND MEN: GOODWOOD

The moose that lived at Goodwood sickened and died.
The Duke's icehouses were inadequate
To keep a body so enormous in
Mild Michaelmas. It was already putrid
When the naturalist-curate trotted over
In dogcart to essay a part-dissection,
Much as he could from high effluvium
Before the corpse had loosened from the bones.
Musing through mask, he cut the animal
Who died without companion. Though they had tried
A male red-deer, such inequality
'A bar to commerce of the amorous kind'
(Or so the curate decorously wrote
To noble amateurs of natural science)
Had left the poor beast lonely. As the stench
Grew insupportable, he gave it up,
Packed instruments, and wrote another letter.
We read it now, and ponder on the moose.

*Personal*

# CONJUNCTION 1980

Three planets stand over our stable,
Jupiter, Saturn, Mars,
All come out of the east
With Venus opposed in the west,
Four together a testament
Of heathenish portent,
Though no one looks or wonders
But we and a few astronomers.
When conjunction glows again
We shall be gone, our children's children
Old, forgetful, unable
To reckon such pallid forebears,
Who lived, bled, loved, and died,
As you and I did, you and I did.

# ABSENCE

When we are parted, the day's despatch
Darkens behind you. The house goes dead.
The muffled birds hide mute in the thatch.
The morning delivers its milk and bread
Unsmiling. Newspapers thud on the mat
In a dull, illegible lump. The stove
Has forgotten the look of food, the cat
Slinks in for statutory meals, not love.
The cups wink heartless along the shelf,
The clock ticks endless with rusty spring.
The telephone squats and huddles itself
In a hunchback crouch, refusing to ring.

These are the moments when I rehearse
The passage of death, my own or yours,
The vanishing point of our universe,
Not merely an absence of miles or hours.

# IMAGININGS

I go to all the places you once loved,
Everywhere lost. I see a smudge of red
Climbing the path ahead,
Reach it at burst of lung; it has not moved;
Only a picnic rag fluttering the bush,
Not your coat's scarlet. In the birdsong hush
I hear alone the tears I have to shed.

I go to all the valleys you once named,
Deep Coombe, Half Moon, and silent Celtic Fields,
Names only. Nothing yields
Your voice to me, no whisper that exclaimed
As deer and fawn came trotting the long ride
With delicate printed track from side to side.
They go, and leave a grief that nothing shields,

The naked grief that keeps an open nerve
To casual promptings, sharp and unaware,
The cold form of the hare,
The circle ash of feathers in the turf,
Empty reminders of the populous day
You made around you, and which shaped the way
We went through time in your unconscious care.

All these imaginings – If you should go
Before me! And if I should leave the first –
Each choice impossibly worst –
And you the one to take the upward, slow,
Trail through the woodland, O I promise you,
With my pale, breathless, tenuous residue,
I shall be trying to reach you, though the heart burst.

# GHOSTS

Ghosts, they tell me, arise
From images too impressed.
The eye absorbs the shape,
Say, of a lantern shade,
Fringed at the base. Later
There walks a crinoline lady,
The retina retaining
Her ebb and flow in flickers
That we call ghostly – though
How headless, bloody spectres
Appear is hard to trace.
Could then some early similar
Implant upon my vision
Make you – a ghost perhaps,
A phantom of recurrence –
And might you too dissolve,
All your dear guidance gone,
The day my eyes are shut?

# WHEN I GROW OLD

When I grow old and mad
Tuck my arm into yours
And walk me round the gardens
Of that sad hospital;
Don't listen to the babble
That drizzles from my lips.
Say something of your own,
A poem, a proverb, a prayer,
To make me half aware
You are still there.

So while my brain contends
With flat-faced Gobi hordes,
The terracotta armies
That horrify in dreams,
Be single, be yourself,
The one trace I can trust
In overlacing forests
Where I have lost all way,
And with each word you say
I shall find day.

# WAKING

I woke with birdsong sun-bewitched,
Turned to begin the day's debate.
Nothing peered through your lashes, stitched
From lid to cheek. In the same state
You lay, still curled, where you had switched
The light off, last night, late.

Horrible liberties life can take
Hammered my heart with human dread.
There seemed no breath. I dared not make
A sound myself. Suddenly you said,
Quick in my arms, 'O, kiss me awake.
I dreamt that you were dead.'

# THE EGG-TIMER

This little V of salt
Is punctual without fault.
Nothing will alter its four-minute warning.
Yolk and albumen feel
The seconds they congeal
Precisely measured every human morning.

Its minor stalactite
Dissolves, grainy and white,
A glacial drift from one globe to the next,
While in the glass below
With stalagmitic flow
A rising cone from nothing resurrects.

This pigmy engine you
Chose for your birthday. True
To that desire, I found our antique symbol.
So now we daily watch
These hemispheres that match
A love that each reverse can reassemble.

## SPRING CLEAN

You bundle from the sunwashed room
A buried winter on your broom,
Augment the annual holocaust
With visitants that time had lost,
The paper body of a moth
Emptied and embalmed by death,
Whole Egypts of the beetle kind
With spider mummies out of mind,
A cenotaph of sheath and shard,
Tenuous topsoil for the yard.

Emerald glitter of the Spring
Welcomes the gift with beak and wing.
Blackbirds, safe in honeysuckle hood,
Darkly intent to nest a brood,
Beady and busy, resurrect
The stuff and spillage you reject,
Tamping and moulding against warm breast
A live shape from the long-dry past,
Simply to make, as make we must,
New loves from debris and from dust.

## IN ARGOLIS

The bubbling, tumbling pan-pipes play.
The shepherd's fingers dance like gnats.
The hoopoe-crested hills stand round
And listen. We leave the white, dust road
To sit in the shade of the gossiping tree,
Each busy branch nudging a neighbour,
While hidden cicadas' sandpaper legs
Ceaselessly sound an eloquent peace.

We know the land was battled over
By beak-faced warriors plated in bronze.
Hercules legend of lion and hydra
Survives in the half-light of violent history.
Yet now the moment is music and love
Unimpaired by so much tragical past;
Lucky alive from our own torn century,
We lie in the cool between thyme and time.

# IN THE CAR PARK

Waiting for you to meet me at the car,
And you not coming, every anxious ghost
Begins to shake and whisper: how you are
Never this much late, have never lost
Your sense of time, have never in the past
Forgotten an appointment, but were there
Before me: could not, at the very most,
Spend half an hour on lengths of linenware.

Panic takes over then. You are not well?
Were knocked down in the street? An ambulance
Is taking you – a stroke? – to hospital?
Who do I telephone? The questions die.
You are here, smiling. 'Sorry. The assistants
Were turning feet to metres.' So was I.

# A SORT OF PERMANENCE

The last bus gone,
The ruby tail-light snaking down,
One extra act of love delaying
The two resigned to walk.
Tangible midsummer dark,
London with scent of flowers,
Breathing from clay-based roses,
Stocks in basement gardens,
No problems on those soft-lit nights
Of linking village-hamlets,
Named Kilburn, Willesden, Notting Hill,
Single police, unarmed, who pace
Unsuspiciously, testing bank and shop,
Safe-deposits all safe.
Not without noise, we pass
All-night parties, lighted windows,
With outward-flapping muslins,
Laughter, a piano, applause,
Urban pleasure, on whose pavement
Violence was shock exception,
Minor larceny made the local news.
Now forty indiscriminate years
Have changed, like wrinkled clusters
We never notice pucker round our eyes,
Our lovewalks into doubts
They ever happened. Yet a tooth-gap
Ago they did, and we, their witnesses,
Remember, a sort of permanence.